TESTIMONIAL

"An easy, informative, and fun read with lots of pragmatic advice for leaders of businesses of all sizes!"

Molly Jungbauer, CPA, CEO of Hollstadt Consulting

"Michelle Jahn's experiences in leading organizations jump out from the pages of this easy-to-read and clearly understandable book. Her thought-provoking questions can assist a CEO (or any leader of a company, group, division, or team) to improve their business operations and achieve a high-quality, sustainable organization for future growth. I would consider this book essential reading for any level of management. I've known Michelle for over thirty years, and the guideposts and suggestions outlined in the book have been fine-tuned from real-life success in her career."

Denis J Muskat, Retired CFO

Make it about THEM, *Then it's all about* YOU!

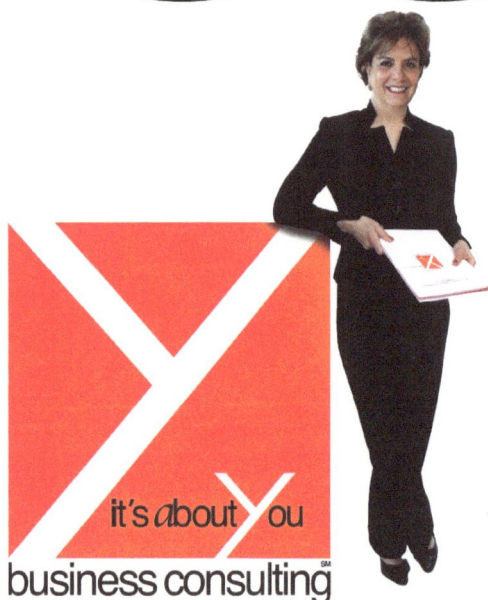

it's *about* you
business consulting℠

Copyright © 2023 It's About You Business Consulting℠, LLC.

ALL RIGHTS RESERVED. This book contains material protected under International and Federal Copyright Laws and Treaties. Any unauthorized reprint or use of this material is prohibited. No part of this book may be reproduced or transmitted in any form or by any means, electronic or mechanical, including photocopying, recording, or by an information storage and retrieval system without express written permission of the author.

ISBN: 979-8-9881660-0-9 (paperback)
ISBN: 979-8-9881660-2-3 (hardback)
ISBN: 979-8-9881660-1-6 (ebook)

TABLE OF CONTENTS

DEDICATION

To my husband, Mark Jahn, an accomplished healthcare management consultant. I admire him for his brilliance, inner strength, and kindness. Together for thirty-four years. His words: "Michelle, it's been a great ride!" Thanks for sharing the journey!

To my son, Trevor Jahn, an aerospace and astronautical engineer and a space mission architect. I admire your tenacity for space exploration and all its opportunities. You inspired me to make the time to complete this book. "Write the book and explore what comes next." Thanks so much!

My mother, the late Irene Headrick Cobb Ballentine, instilled confidence in me to pursue anything and everything without hesitation. She often said, "Solid character and a moral compass are more important than anything. Remember, you will spend a lifetime demonstrating your integrity. A bad choice can make you lose it all overnight. So, protect your character, demonstrate your integrity, treat everyone fairly, and follow that compass. Life is about choices." I continue to share and follow her wisdom.

Thank you to my mentor, the late Raymond Rosedale Jr. MD, a fantastic surgeon and successful financial investor who built several thriving companies. I enjoyed our lunches. When I arrived in town from Chicago, he was eager to share insight into his business investments, hear about my career adventures, and provide me with valuable mentorship. "It's not who you know, Michelle, but who knows you! You must work hard to be acknowledged, respected, and valued in the business." He was right. So very right!

Thank you to my clients and former staff. They valued my leadership and allowed me the opportunity to leave my thumbprint on their organizations and careers. Together, we took on many challenges and made good things happen. More fun is yet to come!

Last, for those who read this book, be thoughtful and willing to act. Yes, you too can make good things happen.

It's about you!

Ready to dive into this? Turn the page.

INTRODUCTION

To be a successful leader, you must establish and maintain
a current business plan and lead the organization
within the guidelines of the plan and its lifecycle.
This book should inspire you to be thoughtful about
your business, the culture you promote, and the value
you provide to all stakeholders. It should challenge
you to change the things within your grasp and
lead with a balance of courage and empathy.

The concept is simple. Life is about choices.
Doing nothing is a choice.
Changing what you can requires effort.
Relationships and people are complex.
To lead a successful business, it's about you.
You must listen and observe, understand market dynamics,
develop a high-energy culture, and deliver your
customers' expectations. Yep, it's all about you!

CHAPTER 1
IT'S YOUR LEADERSHIP

IT'S YOUR BUSINESS!

IT'S YOUR LEADERSHIP! IT'S ABOUT YOU—IT'S
ALL ABOUT YOU!

It's Your Business!

This book is my gift to you. It's about you!

It is short and to the point. You do not have time to read 200 pages, so now it is about you and me. And so, the cycle begins.

In all relationships, it is about the parties involved. But for the next several hours, let's consider the basic premise: **In business, it's about you. Everything in business is about you and the choices you make. Remember, doing nothing is also a choice.**

While the basic premise of this book may sound simplistic, the application can be as straightforward or as complicated as you want it to be. For this to book to be effective, you must be open to change, willing to act, and thoughtful.

It's your business.

It's your leadership.

It's your senior leadership team and their leadership teams.

It's your business plan and strategy.

It's your company culture.

It's the way you approach the market.

It's your vision and innovation.

It's your company's reputation in the market.

It's the way you exceed customers' expectations.

It's your revenue and profitability.

It all begins with you. It is about you!

You want to grow your business and lead a high-energy work environment. You must execute effective company leadership communication and the timeliness of innovation in response to changing market dynamics, deliver internal and external customers' business objectives and expectations, foster a positive company culture, and drive staff development. It's about listening, observing, and a willingness to act.

When you make it about them, it's all about you!

These statements may all sound very basic to you. That is because it is. Many books and webinars about business leadership, company culture, sales, account management, and staffing challenges are available. My business career encompasses executive leadership positions and consulting engagements with Fortune 100, large, well-established, privately owned, and early-stage companies. I have witnessed and experienced numerous business challenges and led successful changes driving improved profits and growth. My observation is, regardless of the size of the company, the challenges remain the same. The bottom line is this: It's all about the basics.

It is simple if you and the leadership team make it simple. Things become complex when you do nothing to change the things that you can. Doing nothing is a choice. It is all about you! If you and the leadership team are honest with yourselves, you know I am right. As I said a few minutes ago, you don't have time to read 200 pages, so let's discuss the basics and focus on how these things impact your business's long-term success and customer relationships. Let's set you and your team up to create companywide awareness to act and effect change where needed to drive tremendous success for your business. It requires diligence, willingness, and communication. Want to dig a little deeper? Stay with me, and let's get started!

It's Your leadership! It's All About you!

You want to drive revenue and profit. You want to retain your customer portfolio and expand into new markets. You may seek increased organic growth and desire to improve customer retention. The company should either maintain or achieve a leadership position in the industry. To do this, you need a current and well-crafted business plan and strategy. You need to understand who cares about the company's products and services, and more importantly, why they care. What's in it for them? Understanding how the products, services, and company culture impact them and their business is essential.

Be thoughtful. Is it easy for customers to do business with your company?

Don't answer that so fast. Think about it. Really, think about it. Would *you* want to do business with your company? Do you know what your company's reputation is in the industry? Is your company known as a great company that consistently delivers on time and is accountable for errors, provides excellent customer service, and has high energy and friendly, well-trained staff focused on gaining customers' loyalty and turning them into brand ambassadors? If so, congratulations. Well done! If not, it's time to investigate. There may be obstacles embedded in company processes—or employees—making it challenging for customers to conduct business with your organization.

It is about the company stakeholders, customers, and employees. That is the key. It is about what they want, their needs, timelines, and the why behind it. How you confirm and exceed those expectations is up to the leadership team and the entire team. **When you make the business's success about them, it will equate to more success.** It's about the business values you establish and the company culture you foster to focus on them.

Let's take a closer look and understand how you can pull together your corporate values and foster a positive culture into a roadmap for success. It begins by establishing and validating the business plan and strategy. Engaging employees in the success of the company's business plan is crucial. In the next two chapters, I share why this matters more than anything to be successful.

CHAPTER 2
IT BEGINS WITH YOUR BUSINESS PLAN

THE BUSINESS PLAN—CURRENT OR MOLDY?

AWARENESS, COMMUNICATION, DISCIPLINE, AND METRICS

This chapter provides executive-level activities that validate the business plan and strategy. It addresses the importance of establishing awareness of the business plan throughout the company and maintaining a disciplined approach to executing the plan.

The Business Plan—Current or Moldy?

The times they are a-changing…

Managing a clearly defined business plan requires a periodic checkup to explore and validate the relevance of the plan and make necessary changes. It is vital to communicate the revised plan to ensure companywide appreciation and awareness and achieve desired results. In Chapter 4, I address the significance of the business lifecycle and customer lifecycle as they apply to the business plan.

Has the leadership team evaluated and updated the business plan to represent the company's response to changes? You may need to address alterations to the longer-term business plan and strategy. Review product lines, and if appropriate, review the results of newly developed or acquired business units, a recent merger or major company acquisition. Did you sell a business unit or product line? Discuss newly developed or altered processes among the leadership team to determine if the changes were temporary or permanent. If your company experienced any of these events, it is time to update the business plan to reflect on investments and changes in strategy and clearly define desired results and timelines.

Regulatory requirements and market changes typically influence business operations, inspire innovation, and affect product readiness timeliness. The ever-changing competitive landscape often creates new business opportunities and requires new service offerings or changes in service delivery to maintain or improve your industry position. If you are experiencing changes in your market, what effect are they having on the short-term and long-term business plan and your strategy? Remember, employees are aware of the competition and constantly hear from recruiters and vendors about new opportunities in your industry. Things often look greener on the other side.

Being successful and retaining the best talent is about communicating expectations and positioning the business appropriately for change. It is about delivering a positive message to move the business forward. Keep employees engaged and confident they are working for a progressive, not a lagging, company. Provide companywide communications regarding the business' response to changes in the market and other forces, such as the impact the economy is having on your business and industry. Lead the company by demonstrating a strong sense of the business plan and establishing a business charter. Simply stated, what is the direction of the company? Do you know where you are headed?

How you navigate and lead during change is critical to business success. Things like mergers, acquisitions, changes in corporate leadership, new market entrants, competitor exits, the impact of the US domestic and global economy, data privacy, security, and advancements in technology, to name a few, can all impact the business and your game plan.

Please invest time in a few valuable exercises. When you are ready, I would like you to complete an assessment that will help you create a general visualization of the dynamics of the business and your leadership team. The purpose is to first gain insight into the current pulse of your business, and then, we address the business plan.

This exercise can be complex. You can reflect on obvious top-of-mind information. Even a short investment of your time will prove insightful. It would be best to reflect on a recent merger, acquisition, new product line, or business unit divestiture for the exercises. If none of these apply to your company, then consider a major event in the market that impacted the business.

Use a whiteboard and do this as a group exercise. Write the following columns: "Pre-Event" (merger acquisition, product line, etc.), "During the Event," and "Current State." Write a short sentence to explain each.

Example: Lack of a business integration plan for a newly acquired business unit or product line resulted in delays in appropriately communicating and engaging with customers and ultimately delayed revenue growth.

You should complete this segment of the exercise in sixty minutes. **Remember, this is a quick, top-of-mind exercise.** We can dig deeper into this another time if you are interested.

	Pre-Event (Merger, New Product, etc.)	During Event	Current State
Business Integration Plan (BIP)			
Revenue			
Profit, Loss			
Investors			
Customers' expectations			
Business Development			
Customer relationship management			

Does your company or a new business unit exist because of a change in market dynamics that presented a business case for your company or new business unit? If that is the situation, create a "Market Conditions" column to list market dynamics and indicators that enabled you to identify the need and the associated business case to launch your new business or business unit. Create a column for "New Business/Current State."

New Business or New Business Unit

	Market Conditions	Current State
List situation for business case		
Size of new business or business unit	N/A	
Industry position	N/A	
Products/ services	N/A	
Growth /Loss	N/A	
Etc.		

If you identified the opportunity to sell a product line or completed a business unit divestiture, that's great. List it!

Business Unit Sale or Divestiture

	Market Opportunity	Current State
Business unit or product		
Conditions for sale		
Eroding customer portfolio		
Timelines for sale		
Etc.		

Once you finish, look at the charts. The visual is impressive. What do you see? A progressive business or a struggling one? How did the company evolve as a result of the event?

It begins with your business plan. Did the senior leadership team work together to innovate and deliver results? Did they put egos and personal goals aside? Did they leverage each of their strengths as a team? Did they demonstrate character and exceptional listening skills?

It is so easy to lead and manage when things are going well. True business leader champions show up during challenging times. What did you learn, and what did the leadership team learn during the events that impacted significant changes in the business? Discuss lessons learned across the company. Yes, please now create lists of the top five things you and the executive team learned about the company, the senior leadership team, and their desire to win and succeed during unprecedented times in the history of the company. Do the following:

Ask each executive team member to list the top five things they learned about the company and place them on the whiteboard.

Top five things each member of the executive team learned about the company culture during unprecedented times:

GRATEFUL WHEN BONUSES WERE PAID

Collaborating and listening to customers enabled necessary changes in service delivery.

FEAR AND LACK OF DEFINITIVE COMMUNICATION DEGRADING EXPECTATIONS CAUSED DISTRACTIONS.

Innovative ideas to remain competitive surfaced from unexpected employees.

EMPLOYEES RALLIED AND WORKED HARDER TO DELIVER RESULTS.

Discuss the results with your team. Look for similarities in the lists and pull together a final list of discoveries. Listen to their comments.

Next, ask each executive team member to list the top five things they observed and learned about the executive team. Review and discuss the observations.

Top five things each member of the executive leadership team learned about the executive leadership team during challenging times.

Strong innovative leaders

Leadership team is no longer territorial – Demonstrated better collaboration.

MADE MISTAKES THAT RESULTED IN LOST REVENUE AND FRUSTRATED CUSTOMERS.

Able to energize the employees and maintain high levels of productivity.

Willing to make hard decisions and implement appropriate actions.

Now, consider the new current state of the business post-event. What is your vision for the future state of the business in the next two to five years? Yep. You guessed it. I want you to create two columns for "Current State" and "Future State." Make the lists. What do you see? Hmmmmmm?

Current State	Future State (2 to 5 years)

If this activity identified the need to further investigate and update the company business plan and strategy, schedule a follow-up session with the leadership team and other appropriate staff to identify gaps and either enhance the existing plan or establish a new plan that can be executed companywide to deliver the desired results.

BUSINESS PLAN AWARENESS, COMMUNICATION, DISCIPLINE, AND METRICS

Did I say business plan?

Sure did, several times. When discussing the details of the customer lifecycle, it is essential to consider the entire business lifecycle. The customer lifecycle begins with the company business plan, which is the foundation for establishing business goals and associated timelines, short-term and long-term roadmaps, and strategies.

What metrics are you using to measure the success of the plan? The business plan must have a near-term and long-term roadmap and strategy. Is the company achieving milestones as planned? How is that monitored? The business development, marketing, and business relationship management staff must understand and follow the roadmap and deliver results within the plan's required timelines. Do they pursue business relationships within the guidelines of the plan?

Confirm the target market and create a profile of the best customers to pursue. Validation of the ideal customer profile is imperative. Engage several members of the executive team sales, account management operations, and product development organizations to share their ideas regarding the best customer profiles to pursue. Once you gain consensus, then validate and communicate the final profiles. Remember, the largest customers may not be the best customers.

Does the sales staff seek customers that meet the criteria for your best customer profile? Are the sales executives, account executives, and engagement managers collaborating to ensure positive customer experiences? Are you confident they are creating a desired customer portfolio that can evolve with the business?

Selling and creating new business relationships beyond the scope of current operational processes without prior internal collaboration with the delivery team to ensure a successful and timely outcome for the customer can disrupt the business and customer lifecycle. Is the sales organization functioning beyond the scope of the business plan to drive revenue but eroding profits and causing internal challenges across business verticals?

Take a deep breath. Think about it and validate the answers with your teams.

Keeping a pulse on sales metrics and the impact on delivery and internal operations is essential. We all know the sales team drives revenue. However, an undisciplined sales organization can cause havoc with the business plan's success, create issues with the operations team, and ultimately lead to unhappy customers.

We often hear sales organizations drive product development. That works well when there is a process for innovation and product development. Comparatively, the sales organization can cause problems when promises are made to customers without thought or internal collaboration to validate capabilities and timely delivery.

Do you have an innovation review process for acceptance and inclusion in the business plan? Is the operations team interacting with the innovation team and sales organization to plan for appropriate changes in processes and delivery? Or is your operations team rigid and unwilling to establish new procedures to support the business plan long term? If that is the case, it's time to investigate why. In Chapter 3, we dig a little deeper into your process for leading innovation and cultivating staff ideas into new product initiatives that can create profitable revenue and enhance your market position.

A timely and concise internal communications program that supports an evolving business plan, new product launches, and changing market dynamics can energize employees and avoid internal politics that often create obstacles. Timely communication regarding changes in the plan is essential to reduce distractions and maintain appropriate levels of focus among the employees. Remember, ambiguity breeds doubt, causes confusion regarding clarity of purpose, and promotes negative employee energy. Do you cultivate an environment that keeps employees focused on the plan, producing desired results to achieve stakeholder value?

Confident in your thoughtful answers? Let's do a quick checkup for discovery regarding the validity of the business plan.

Consider the exercises you completed earlier regarding the impact of a new business acquisition, new product line launch, or business unit divestiture. Has the leadership team revisited the business plan within the past twenty-four months and modified the plan based on the impact of rapidly changing market dynamics? If the answer is yes, then is the revised business plan documented? If so, where is it located? Who has access to the plan? Is it in a password-protected file with only executive leadership access? Do all employees understand how they participate in the success or failure of the plan?

If the answer is no, the leadership team has not revisited the business plan in the last twenty-four months, then the plan is at risk of being outdated and ineffective based on current market conditions. An obsolete or undisciplined plan can cause a loss of market position and missed opportunities. Maintaining a disciplined approach to following the business plan prevents distractions, avoids ambiguity among staff, and ensures the sales and account management organizations focus on developing and retaining a customer portfolio that supports the current and future state of the business. These critical success factors maintain the foundation of the business strategy, growth, and profitability.

Consider adding the following discussion topics to the agendas of your executive staff meetings to test their knowledge and the validity of the plan:

- Is everyone aware of the business plan? You may be surprised to discover only some on the leadership team are aware of the details of the plan. If there was a recent change in executive leadership, it is time to discuss the plan to validate the current and future state of the business with everyone on the team and ensure they are focused on the new plan.

- Do you offer a hybrid workplace, enabling some staff to work offsite and others are required to work in the office? Has this resulted in productivity challenges? Are you considering harvesting real estate to eliminate the costs of maintaining empty buildings? Employee communication regarding current and future expectations regarding workspace is critical to set employee expectations. Many large and small companies are considering selling their real estate or not renewing commercial leases. For example, faced with the challenges of owning a large corporate building and an evolving hybrid work environment, Baxter International placed the corporate headquarters facility and the 101-acre campus in a northern Chicago suburb for sale in May 2022. The corporate headquarters is a significant architectural landmark in the Chicagoland area. Unused buildings are a drag on the business. Have you determined your facilities plan and strategy short term and long term?

- Has the approach to communicating and meeting with your customers changed in the past twenty-four months? Are you meeting at the customer campus, traveling across the US and international markets, or conducting virtual meetings? Discuss the modifications made to customer interactions and how these modifications impact budgets and delivery timelines. How is technology supporting the sales organization?

- Market changes and evolving customer needs often create opportunities in new geographic markets within and outside the US. Consider the possibilities.

- Review similarities in changing customer expectations and the underlying causes. Are the changes impacting your industry or specific to your business?

- What impacted the product and service delivery now offered by your competitors?

- Explore staffing and skill requirements to support the business plan and strategy. Determine if current staffing skills need to be improved to support the plan longer term. Is new talent acquisition included in the plan? If so, will that be accomplished by a business unit acquisition or direct staff recruitment?

- It is common knowledge that acquisitions can disrupt company culture. Listening and communicating with the staff is vital to avoid a toxic work environment if an investment or purchase is in the plan. You are most likely nodding your head in agreement. So, if an acquisition is in the foreseeable future, what is your plan for integrating company cultures to avoid erosion and doubt among staff?

Based on the discussion among the executive team and the previous whiteboard exercises, you may discover it is time to pause, evaluate, and recalibrate the business plan for clarity and purpose. Evaluate the plan to reconfirm targeted milestones, continued growth, and stakeholder value. Review market dynamics, reconfirm your target market and customer's expectations, and evaluate products and services. Reviewing the supporting business operations model can provide insight into inefficiencies and highlight operational successes.

Remember to celebrate successful operational functions, new sales achieved within the guidelines of the plan, and organic revenue growth. Success instills positive energy among staff and promotes a confident, energized culture.

Evaluate changes to your customer portfolio. Discuss customer portfolio changes with your business relationship management team and review customer trends. The business plan should address evolving customer expectations and define projected changes in the customer portfolio. Customer acquisitions, retention, and growth should be on track to achieve desired revenue and profits in current and future years. Modifications to customer relationship management may be necessary to ensure customer retention and profitable growth. Review customer management processes to ensure your organization understands and supports customer goals and objectives appropriately.

Document competition changes and highlight new industry standards that affect operations and product development. Changes in product requirements, regulatory requirements, and customer needs can directly impact operations, technology needs, implementation processes, timelines, and margins. Remember, market dynamics and customer expectations can impact business functions—and the business plan.

Have you created new products and services and discontinued others? If so, these changes can impact sales, operations, and the client portfolio.

Last and more importantly, who knows and understands the plan? Beyond the executive leadership team, do the employees know and understand the basics of the revised plan? Have you communicated the plan to the entire leadership team, all stakeholders, and employees companywide? As mentioned previously, are they confident in their degree of understanding of the significance each of their positions plays in supporting the success of the plan? If not, how can you motivate them and impact company culture to focus on them and their performance against the plan? No, I am not referring to annual employee performance reviews. I am referring to instilling daily pride and confidence in one's work and interaction with internal and external customers to help them achieve their business goals and objectives.

Yes, components of the plan may be on a need-to-know basis. You may be involved in discussions regarding a merger, acquisition, or a unique project that you are not ready to share with the general staff. These things can be sensitive information. I am not talking about those initiatives. Does the entire company have a clear understanding of the plan? Consider this scenario: If I asked random employees to tell me about the company's business plan and how their positions support its success or failure, would they be able to explain to me with enough detail to demonstrate they understand the plan and have pride in the job position they hold in the company?

Employees should understand the goals and metrics used by the company and its customers to measure the success of key customer relationships. Can employees articulate customers' business needs and how your company helps customers achieve their business goals today and in the future? Do they know the strategy and vision for significant accounts within their books of business? Would the business development, business relationship management, marketing, and proposals teams be able to answer the question with an appropriate amount of detail to demonstrate they are pursuing only desired business relationships?

Would they answer the question by providing the primary target markets and stating the easiest products and services to sell? Sales and account management staff may know which products or services yield the highest revenue and can name the customers that produce the most revenue within their books of business. I would like to know what the operations staff would say about their knowledge of the plan and how their positions and processes support the effectiveness of the plan. Can the operations staff articulate the significance of the reliability of downstream vendors that support effective product and service delivery? Can they tell me how a vendor failure can impact the successful execution of the company business plan, or would they simply say that a vendor failure would affect product production and or service delivery? Do they know how a downstream vendor failure could impact the company's customer relationships, revenue, and profits? Awareness of the business continuity plans (BCP) designed to avoid vendor disruption and protect customer service delivery is important. There may be a BCP regarding vendor failures, but when was the last time the staff reviewed it for potential updates?

Can the IT staff embellish how technology supports the business plan for the current and future state of the business? Can HR articulate the significance of the plan as it relates to effective talent acquisition and retention of a well-balanced staff portfolio to support the current and desired future state of the business?

So, why is it essential for the employees to understand and be able to describe the business plan and their role in supporting the plan?

CHAPTER 3
CULTURE

COMPANY CULTURE AND INNOVATION

COMPANY CULTURE—IT'S ABOUT THEM!

Company culture can impact the success or failure of the business plan and strategy. This chapter discusses the importance of fostering a high-energy culture driven by honest communication, timely innovation, and the impact of new product launches or a business unit divestiture. Understanding the significance of individual contributions to achieve the efficient execution of the business plan and desired results is vital to supporting a positive culture.

COMPANY CULTURE AND INNOVATION

Have you fostered a company culture that embraces change and promotes innovation? Who owns innovation within your company? Do you have a product development team and specialists to work on this? Or do you engage the entire company to offer innovative ideas and business plans for consideration? What is the innovation submission process? **It's about them! And when you make it about them...**

They do the work. They are productive every day, collaborating with clients and vendors. They are the eyes and ears of the company. They see and experience, up close and personal, the impact of changing market dynamics and customer needs. Have you fostered a business culture that encourages and empowers staff to submit product and service ideas supported by their innovative business plans? You have a tremendous amount of intellectual capital engaged daily across the company. Remember, every position is essential, and those who do the work engage with customers and prospects. They may surprise you. They may have the best ideas for new products or services.

You are responsible for getting people jazzed about submitting ideas and being engaged in the future of the business. Once your team embraces a new product or service idea, you must initiate steps to breathe new life into the business plan.

Yes, back to that business plan.

If you release new products or services soon or in the future, did you appropriately review and communicate the new products and services companywide? Did you instill excitement or create anxiety among the employees? Of course, the executive leadership team effectively shared the new associated sales and revenue goals. What about the other details? Are you sunsetting any products or services? If so, what is the timeline? How can the discontinuation of a product line or services impact employees and their positions? Suppose I talked to random employees across the company. Could they tell me about the changes to the business plan and how sunsetting a product or service may impact their position and productivity? Are they confident in their understanding regarding the game plan within the next twelve months and how this will impact customer relationships and the future of the company?

Remember, positive energy creates more positive energy. People like to feel that they are part of a progressive company moving forward. They must also understand how new products or service lines impact their job and expected performance metrics. Considering the overall impact of internal processes and inter-departmental co-dependencies is crucial. While this may seem obvious, you may be surprised how companies fail to deliver a timely message to employees to circumvent gossip and incorrect assumptions. Coffee talk can be damaging to staff morale and the business. Best to be in control of the message. Honesty and appropriate positioning make a difference in employees' perceptions of company leadership and their understanding of the future of the business and their roles in the company.

As I mentioned, how did eliminating a product or service impact current processes? How did a new product or service impact internal and external processes? Have you implemented changes in domestic and global travel policies? If so, how? What policies and procedures did the company implement to support business development and business relationship management staff to enable them to deliver the necessary sales, retention, and organic growth goals? What technology is in place to support their needs?

Company Culture – It's About them!

Yes, company culture can impact the success or failure of the plan.

Too often, there is a perception that high-profile positions are more critical than others. Often, staff needs to recognize the significance of their work, and more importantly, why their role and contributions matter when it comes to impacting the success or failure of the plan. Do you promote a culture celebrating achievements and milestones within departments and business units? Remember, success breeds more success. People want to work for companies that have positive energy and demonstrate staff appreciation.

If I took a walk through the halls of your company, would I see people with smiles on their faces who are actively collaborating with peers? Would I feel an atmosphere of excitement? Or would I witness a heads-down atmosphere filled with tension and anxiety? These polar-opposite scenarios do exist; I have seen them. How would you label your atmosphere in the office and during online virtual meetings?

People will not always remember everything you said, but they will remember how you made them feel.

Consider the corporate/executive office, operations, sales, and account management environments. Is arrogance among individuals in revenue-producing or senior management positions causing others in the company to feel less significant? Do staff feel comfortable discussing roadblocks and challenges in daily job functions? Do you foster a culture where staff can readily communicate process inefficiencies impacted by inter-department co-dependencies? Do staff feel comfortable engaging and leading discussions that improve inter-departmental performance and the impact on the success of the plan?

Does your leadership team work together to integrate their vertical departments and improve co-dependencies? Does the staff understand the importance of downstream vendors and their impact on the operations of the company and the plan? Do they seek better ways to function with downstream vendors to support the timely execution and delivery of your products and services?

Are business unit verticals under executive leadership working together to retain and enhance customer relationships? It may be time to explore departmental co-dependencies and examine cross-functional collaboration and the timeliness of internal and external deliverables.

Discuss this openly with the executive leadership team and engage in an exercise to uncover the hidden truths within the organization and identify opportunities to impact change.

Each senior leader should consider the value and impact of individuals working within their vertical and the impact the success or failure of each position and individual's performance can have on the success or failure of the business plan. A meaningful attempt at this activity should take one to two days to complete companywide. Before launching this exercise, the executive leadership team may indicate they already have this information in HR reports and performance evaluations. Reports are different from the same level of awareness I want you to establish with this exercise.

Request a more detailed awareness among the organization's leadership about the positions and the people who sit in those chairs. They most likely know their direct reports well. They should dig deeper into their vertical organizations to meet with staff in their work environments, whether on campus or online, if they have remote staff. Before you begin, review and discuss the significance of this exercise with the leadership team.

Ask your team to explore and answer the question, "Why is it important for everyone to understand the business plan and how their role impacts the success of the plan?"

Please encourage them to think about every position within the company. Before you start, I provided a few examples to stimulate thoughtful discussion among executive leaders. The examples should help start the dialog among your leaders before beginning the exercise.

1. US Postal Carriers, Amazon, UPS, and FedEx delivery staff are essential downstream vendors that support businesses and consumers by delivering various items, including office supplies, product parts, household goods, healthcare products, prescription drugs, and other items nationwide. With truck drivers, courier services, and delivery staff, to name a few, many businesses and consumer needs are met. How could the delivery delay of your company's products and services impact your business relationships with your customers? What was or could the impact be on revenue, profits, and customer retention? How did or could delivery delays impact the health and well-being of consumers?

2. Consider the significance of healthcare benefits configuration teams, specifically pharmacy benefits coders. They are responsible for accurate code and entering pharmacy benefit plan designs and drug formularies into pharmacy benefit management (PBM) adjudication systems to ensure precise pharmacy claims adjudication. Pharmacy benefits entered correctly into a PBM adjudication system are considered good work. Consumers receive the right drug for the right price

at the right time. Prescription drug adherence is vital to effective treatment for acute and chronic illnesses. When pharmacy benefit coders make mistakes, the errors can impact the accurate and timely delivery of pharmacy services and healthcare treatment outcomes. Errors can also affect PBM revenue and pharmacy payments. Identified errors can result in penalties costing a PBM millions of dollars in performance guarantees and result in the development and implementation of corrective action plans (CAPS). Benefit coding errors can cause a customer to take their PBM business out to bid, placing the PBM contract renewal at risk and disrupting the lifecycle of the business relationship.

In reflecting on this example, the role of Pharmacy Benefits Configuration Coders significantly impacts PBM revenue, profits, clinical care, consumer satisfaction, and client relationships. What role do they play in the customer lifecycle? A significant one. Seldom acknowledged for the work they perform, PBM coders have a thankless position.

When you open the dialog with the senior leadership team and create an environment to acknowledge the relevance of each position within the company, your team and employees will understand the success of the business plan is about each of them recognizing the importance of their job and the work they perform to achieve company milestones, metrics, and satisfied customers. **And when you make it about them…!**
It's about the company culture you foster and the leadership you demonstrate daily through your actions.
I highly recommend you schedule a week of review to engage with each business unit leader and their business unit verticals. Clear off your calendar, walk the halls, and talk to your manufacturing and production staff. Talk to the

implementation staff and ask them about their challenges and successes. Talk to individual employees, remote or on campus, and understand their roles and responsibilities. Surprise them by taking a chair beside them on their side of the desk. Ask what they are working on and discuss how they support the business plan. You may be surprised at what you discover. They will be impressed you care. Best to avoid scheduling the dialog with them, just show up unexpectedly.

By the way, the first time I did this, I let the managers know I would meet with employees to learn about their positions and their work. Unbeknownst to me, the managers talked to their employees ahead of time and instructed them on what they should tell me. I soon realized my mistake. In the future, whether with my staff or clients, I always made these visits unannounced and randomly selected the employees I wanted to meet without manager involvement. The outcome and the dialogues were much better and had a better impact.

You may be thinking you do not have time to do this. **You need to make time to do this!** You will learn more by interacting with employees at all organizational levels than by receiving reports during executive staff meetings. I have done this exercise in both publicly traded corporations and privately held organizations. Each time I have done this, I discovered things. I identified processes that were old and needed revisions. I learned about unreported successes and staff who were quietly satisfied and productive in their work environment. I heard very innovative ideas and saw the excitement in the employee's eyes.

I heard from people frustrated by co-dependencies on other departments, often impacting the timely delivery of their customer commitments.

Following the employee interactions, I recommended and executed the implementation of annual business process improvement initiatives (BPI) and witnessed company cultures playing a significant role in effective process improvement. The outcome positively impacted both internal and external levels of client satisfaction. I discuss BPI more in Chapter 6.

So, now that we have established the importance of everyone's role in supporting the business plan's success, does the leadership team agree that everyone plays a vital role in sustaining and growing the business?

The Business Plan. Three powerful words establish the foundation for client lifecycle management: the business plan. Clarity and success of the business plan begin with leadership focus and commitment. **It starts with you making it about them.**

Chapter 4
Customer Lifecycle Management

Significance of Business and Customer Lifecycle Models

Create Your Unique Models

This chapter addresses the value of the business and customer lifecycles as they apply to the business plan. Developing models that represent lifecycles unique to your business is essential to establish accountability for all parties involved in successful customer lifecycle management and delivery of the business plan.

Significance of Business and Customer Lifecycles

Creating the customer lifecycle model for your business is an important exercise that provides visualization of segment complexities and establishes internal and external customer expectations, accountabilities, and timelines. The following scenario demonstrates the importance of understanding and creating a unique model that represents your business.

A few years ago, I received a call from a CFO for a Pharmacy Benefit Management (PBM) company. He asked that I meet with the CEO while he was in Chicago to discuss their customer lifecycle because they had challenges with customer retention. During the meeting, the CEO quickly told me they had a great sales organization. They were closing sales fast and bringing in lots of new business. "But as fast as we are onboarding new customers, we are losing them out the bottom." He was convinced he did not have a sales problem; they had a customer lifecycle problem. He asked me to establish a customer lifecycle model to improve customer retention. I agreed to the engagement, but only if I could conduct a 45-day assessment of the sales, implementation, and account management organizations and their processes. He agreed.

The outcome was indisputable. **The company did have a sales problem and an account management problem.** Customer losses were the direct result of an undisciplined sales process and a lack of knowledge transfer across the company regarding expectations sold to the customers. They needed a consistent approach to managing customer relationships. The sales organization frequently promised services beyond the current scope of business operations. In essence, they were committing to customize benefits offerings without consideration of IT limitations and other internal operational challenges.

There needed to be more knowledge transfer from the sales executives to the implementation team. There was a delay in the engagement of the assigned account executives. The implementation team needed a clearer understanding of what was sold and committed to deliver to the customers. Without the knowledge transfer, they assumed there were no custom requirements and the standard implementation project requirements and schedule would be appropriate. Once the implementation team was deep into the project, they would uncover customer expectations not in the project plan. Staff struggled and worked long hours to deliver on customer expectations within the designated timeline before going live, and customers were frustrated. Consistency in the timeliness of contract completions needed to be improved. Unfortunately, this presented opportunities for customers to continue negotiations and request performance guarantees not previously discussed during the sale.

Many customers were ready to seek another PBM shortly after they were live with the new Pharmacy Benefits Program. Account executives were trying to manage and retain unhappy customers who needed more confidence in the team assigned to their accounts. To make things worse, they did not have a clearly defined account management process to grow and retain customers. The account teams needed training and coaching. Each department within the PBM organization acted within its silos without regard to how this behavior impacted customer satisfaction, retention, and operations. There were many swirling and operational redundancies to get the work done. The lack of a process with clearly defined account management accountability created obstacles to forecasting organic growth and budgeting.

The executive staff was both pleased with the assessment and, in several aspects, surprised with the discovery details. I was retained by the CEO for an additional six months to collaborate with staff to develop a robust customer lifecycle model that represented their business and improved customer retention. I established account executive books of business review meetings with the executive team, and I led the re-organization of their account management organization, implementing processes across the organization and assigning accountability for customer retention and growth. The new customer lifecycle model included a well-defined segment for the sales process and required the engagement of the appointed account executive before implementation. Embedded in the model was a formal process for knowledge transfer from the sales organization to the implementation team and assigned account executive. The customer lifecycle model was rolled out companywide to establish awareness and understanding regarding departmental roles and responsibilities.

Recognizing the need for a consistent methodology and much-needed training for the account team, I recommended the Miller Heiman Large Account Management Process (LAMP®). We embedded LAMP® in the customer lifecycle model and required all account executives to utilize the LAMP® methodology. LAMP® gave the account management organization a consistent language and process for understanding, managing, and growing complex customer relationships. The customer lifecycle model included the methodology. Two years later, I received a call from the CFO. He validated that the customer lifecycle model worked, and client retention had improved immensely.

CREATE YOUR UNIQUE MODELS

If you have a visual representation of your customer lifecycle recognized by the entire organization—great!

If not, creating your business's customer lifecycle model diagram provides immediate visualization and accountability for all stakeholders. Each lifecycle segment represents processes and metrics to monitor progress against milestones. It is important to note the customer lifecycle resides with the company's business lifecycle.

That is great if you have a visual representation of your customer lifecycle. Review the templates on the following pages if you still need to establish the model. I embedded a few items within each segment as examples. The illustrations do not represent all aspects within each segment, nor do they represent your unique business model. Visualizing your customer lifecycle is a valuable tool during company townhall meetings as a reminder to employees of the lifecycle segments' significance and role in the customer lifecycle. Sharing the model with customers can be beneficial in establishing expectations for both organizations when onboarding new accounts.

Optimizing the business lifecycle to drive results

Plan discipline

Clarity of purpose, mission, and vision set the stage for a well-crafted business plan, one that defines growth, creates compelling product/sevice offerings, identifies target markets, integrates the ideal staffing model, and establishes stakeholder expectations. When executed with diligence, it delivers results.

The handshake

Getting the handshake, that signed contract, is the culmination of plan discipline. It's the result of training, coaching, prospecting, setting expectations, negotiating, and closing the deal—setting in motion the next phase of the customer relationship....and the moment of truth begins.

Delivering the goods

Fulfilling customer expectations is both the goal and responsibility of the entire organization. To succeed, every detail of the sales promise—every expectation held by the new customer—must be shared and undestood by all. Customer expectations shape an implementation plan with details of management responsi-bilities, accountability, timelines, and quality.

Build and bond

Like any successful relationship, customers need nurturing. These relationships must be based on understanding customer goals, recognizing evolving business requirements, and continuous collaboration over time. Interactions based on these foundational principles produce loyalty, customer retention, and business growth.

Renew and recommit

Cultivating long-term customer relationships and delivering expected results creates Brand Ambassadors, secures critical corporate assets, and enhances stakeholder value.

Customer Lifecycle

Business Lifecycle Example

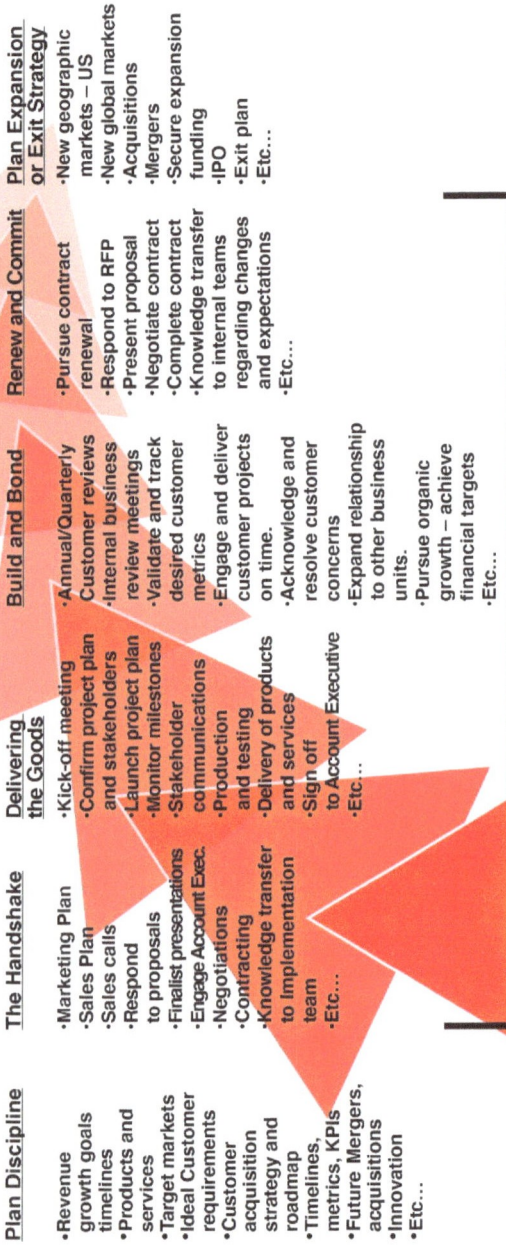

Plan Discipline	The Handshake	Delivering the Goods	Build and Bond	Renew and Commit	Plan Expansion or Exit Strategy
•Revenue growth goals timelines	•Marketing Plan	•Kick-off meeting	•Annual/Quarterly Customer reviews	•Pursue contract renewal	•New geographic markets – US
•Products and services	•Sales Plan	•Confirm project plan and stakeholders	•Internal business review meetings	•Respond to RFP	•New global markets
•Target markets	•Sales calls	•Launch project plan	•Validate and track desired customer metrics	•Present proposal	•Acquisitions
•Ideal Customer requirements	•Respond to proposals	•Monitor milestones	•Engage and deliver customer projects on time.	•Negotiate contract	•Mergers
•Customer acquisition strategy and roadmap	•Finalist presentations	•Stakeholder communications	•Acknowledge and resolve customer concerns	•Complete contract	•Secure expansion funding
•Timelines, metrics, KPIs	•Engage Account Exec.	•Production and testing	•Expand relationship to other business units.	•Knowledge transfer to internal teams regarding changes and expectations	•IPO
•Future Mergers, acquisitions	•Negotiations	•Delivery of products and services	•Pursue organic growth – achieve financial targets	•Etc....	•Exit plan
•Innovation	•Contracting	•Sign off to Account Executive	•Etc....		•Etc....
•Etc...	•Knowledge transfer to Implementation team	•Etc...			
	•Etc...				

Customer Lifecycle

CHAPTER 5
PROTECTING CORPORATE ASSETS

LEADERSHIP AND PLAN DISCIPLINE

THE HANDSHAKE—THE MOMENT OF TRUTH

WHO OWNS CUSTOMER RELATIONSHIPS?

TEAM COACHING YIELDS
HIGH-PERFORMANCE RESULTS

A WELL-BALANCED CUSTOMER PORTFOLIO

This chapter addresses how your leadership and adherence to the business plan can solidify customer relationships through a team-oriented process to create a critical, tangible corporate asset and significantly increase the value of your organization.

Leadership and Plan Discipline

Like the coach of a sports team, the CEO is responsible for developing pride in ownership and instilling a sense of loyalty within the team. Exceeding business plan milestones is like a sports team achieving a championship or breaking a record. Every member of the team is essential. The team must work together to win. After all, the business plan's success depends upon the leadership team's cohesiveness. It's about them. Keeping them focused on the short-term and long-term outcomes of the business plan is not easy. It requires a disciplined approach to leading the business and making tough decisions to drive results.

A disciplined approach to following the business plan is often lost based on leadership's focus to "just make the numbers." Before pursuing new sales, the opportunities should be vetted and aligned with the company's business plan. Establishing the foundation for accountability between the parties pursuing new sales and those managing complex business relationships is essential to sustain customer longevity and revenue growth.

Suppose the executive sales leader is struggling to make the target revenue for the quarter. In that case, they are responsible for investigating the issue within the sales organization vertical and addressing the impact on the business plan with their executive leadership peers. Have regulatory requirements within the industry changed, causing concern among customers? New guidance for staff training and looming operational changes can impact the sales timeline. What is happening within the competitive landscape? Are existing products and services meeting evolving customer and regulatory needs? It may be a seasonal situation and possible to generate more revenue later. There can be a sales staff or sales coaching issue.

Sales team coaching is critical and often not provided by sales leaders, primarily because many sales leaders are not good coaches and invest less than adequate time in the field, providing their team with valuable feedback and coaching. I will address the importance of effective sales coaching and call planning in more detail later in this chapter. Together, these various scenarios cross over and impact multiple executive leader verticals, including but not limited to sales, marketing, innovation, product development, and operations.

When you make it about them and foster an integrated leadership culture, the leadership team will collaborate to identify solutions that either support the business plan or determine appropriate and timely revisions, potentially opening the door for product development, acquisition, or merger opportunities.

The leadership team must recognize their loyalty to the company begins with their commitment to each other across the leadership team. Loyalty starts at the top of the organization. While this sounds simplistic and is not rocket science, the truth is businesses struggle because executive leadership and the leadership in their vertical organizations are not working together. A leadership team that becomes territorial will not function well. When territorial distractions break up the cohesiveness of the leadership team, the outcome results in increased operational costs, loss of revenue, profits, and customers. Key staff begin to exit the company. With the exit of employees, the intellectual capital walks right out the door and goes to the competition, or they become the competition by starting their own business. When leaders lose their focus on the team's cohesiveness and begin protecting their vertical organization…well, things get ugly, and often, client expectations become secondary. Sound familiar? If you have enjoyed working for more than one organization, you may have repeatedly witnessed this phenomenon.

When it becomes less about client expectations and delivering a successful outcome for the overall business plan, and more about individual senior leaders' goals and egos, it impacts both short-term and long-term company revenue and profits. It can affect the company's position and reputation in the industry and the markets you serve. Remember, your reputation in the industry impacts client acquisition, client retention, and staff recruitment. These things matter if you want to hire and retain exceptional talent to maintain a leadership position in the industry. To be sure we have a clear understanding, consider the following.

The importance of consistency and a disciplined approach to the execution of the business plan is critical.

By now, you are beginning to understand that the business's success is making it about them, so it is all about you. Deviating beyond the rails of the business plan without cause is disruptive and can prove to be quite costly. It would be best if you establish a culture focused on following the guidelines of the plan (achieving new sales revenue, profits, pursuing ideal customers, etc.) and the ability to deliver clients' expectations. That takes discipline and the willingness to walk away from business opportunities that can disrupt the business. Communicating the business plan companywide and establishing goals, objectives, metrics, and milestones that support the plan is essential for monitoring progress and providing the necessary leadership to execute the plan. I continue to underscore the concept that everyone should understand the significance of their position and their contribution's impact on the business plan's success. What metrics have you and your team established to monitor progress? Do you conduct companywide employee meetings each quarter that provide insight into the YTD short-term and long-term success of the plan? Do employees understand their contribution eventually impacts financial reports and business metrics? No, I am not kidding. Everyone must understand their role in achieving the required results to support the success of the plan, not just the metrics for their departments.

I distinctly remember meeting with a newly recruited account executive and sharing insight into the significance of her book of business and its impact on the company's desire for geographic expansion as defined in the business plan. She had several customers who were expected to expand their businesses into new markets within the next two years. Securing renewed contracts would support organic growth and expansion in the targeted geographic regions. Loss of those contract renewals would cause a significant reduction in revenue and create a challenge for expansion in the desired geographic area. Creating awareness regarding the significance of her book of business in the company's future geographic expansion was important.

Ultimately, she focused her efforts on collaborating with the customer's leadership teams regarding the company's desire to expand into its target markets. As a result, both organizations worked together to develop roadmaps for success, and the pending contract renewals were successfully completed. This elevated her book of business significantly and established it as one of the fastest growing books of business within the company.

It was shocking to me when she later shared that her previous employer had not provided insight into the impact of her book of business on their business plan. Wow!

THE HANDSHAKE—THE MOMENT OF TRUTH

When a salesperson sells a product or service without alignment with the customer's business needs and expectations, the result can be costly in the short term and long term. It is important to remember those impacted by the product or service delivery have specific business and personal expectations. It is easy to overlook the details and need a complete understanding of the customer's expectations. We all know satisfied customers have an increased propensity to purchase more products and services. They are also more likely to renew the contract term and continue the business relationship.

The foundation of a building is critical to the quality and longevity of its structure. The same comparison is true for business relationships. Align sales opportunities with the company's business plan. As previously discussed, all customer relationships are corporate assets that either add value or create a drag on the business. Engaging in business opportunities that add value to the bottom line and the company's position within the industry is important. During the sales process, confirming the customer's expectations and understanding the goals and objectives of a newly formed business relationship define the foundation for trust and longevity. Once a sale is complete, the process quickly transitions from pursuing a prospect to nurturing and building a relationship to benefit both organizations. Disseminate contractual details within the selling organization. Communicate the goals and objectives of both the customer and the selling organization. Effective communication provides the basis for clearly defined metrics and timelines for measuring and viewing success by both organizations. Engaging the business relationship manager, account management team, operations staff, and ancillary departments early in understanding the goals and objectives of a complex business relationship enhances the probability of creating a long-term brand ambassador. **And the moment of truth begins!**

Do you have a process to review business plan alignment with new sales opportunities? How is success defined and measured by your organization when reviewing customer relationships? Who is accountable for the retention and growth of new business relationships? How does your company transition from the handshake to the moment of truth?

WHO OWNS CUSTOMER RELATIONSHIPS?

It is important to focus on the value you bring to customer relationships. Are customers excited to meet with your leadership team, account executives, and engagement managers to discuss their recommendations? If so, well done. You must be delighted to have achieved this customer respect and collaboration level.

Do customers value their business relationships with your organization and view it as an asset to their business, or are your products and services merely a commodity they can obtain from your competition? If you are operating a commodity-type business, it's even more vital to demonstrate value to your customers to ensure contract retention and organic growth.

Are existing relationships profitable, merely break even, or strategic, enabling penetration into new geographic markets? Developing a customer portfolio that mirrors the expected outcome of your short-term and long-term business plan is an ongoing process that requires discipline, awareness, and metrics. Sales and marketing teams focused on pursuing ideal customers and business opportunities according to the business plan are the first to be accountable for driving long-term plan results. Suppose they are focusing on merely hitting revenue targets without consideration for building long-term relationships. In that case, they are missing the mark and creating a pot that will eventually boil over and make a mess. It is crucial to enter relationships with eyes wide open. Onboarding a customer beyond the rails of the business plan will eventually have issues, which I have witnessed many times. As discussed in the previous chapter, undisciplined sales organizations can be responsible for disruption to the business and client lifecycles.

What do you know about your most significant customer relationships, not just the revenue generated by those key business relationships but why those customers are doing business with your organization and how your products or services support the success of their business plans? Validation of your customer's short-term and long-term business goals—and, more importantly, the impact your products and services have on supporting their business objectives—can impact projected revenue growth and margin. Suppose the company's business plan includes a timeline for the retirement of any products, services, or the sale of a company division or business unit. How will that impact customers and your employees?

Customer relationships are corporate assets to be protected and valued. Suppose I asked your staff to tell me the value your organization brings to enhance the business relationships with your key customers. Would they be able to answer confidently? Could they tell me the role they play in supporting customer relationships? Do they understand the significance of the work they perform each day to secure the longevity and growth of your business?

Consider this. I am sure you can think of your largest and most valuable customers. I would be surprised if you are not acutely aware of the direct impact the loss of those assets would have on the business, not only financially but how the loss would impact your position in the industry. Imagine how the loss of a few significant customers could create an image that your business can no longer sustain large accounts, opening the door for the competition to pursue additional customers within your portfolio and creating challenges for new customer acquisition. Comparatively, acquisitions of large accounts can also dramatically impact your industry position. Companywide recognition that customer relationships are significant corporate assets to be protected is important for business plan success.

Monitor significant customer relationships to achieve desired results. Are you engaging annually with your key customers to validate the expected performance of their business relationships, reconfirming your understanding of their business needs, and providing valuable recommendations? In addition to creating deeper business relationships, annual customer review meetings can create opportunities for organic growth, enable better sales forecasting and budgeting, provide insight into new opportunities for innovation and product development, and push timelines based on their critical business needs.

Customers that utilize significant staff time are labor intensive and may yield low revenue and profits. Are those customers still viable for the growth and longevity of your business? Make hard decisions to change your customer portfolio by developing plans to fire those customers. (Yes, I *did* say that.)

Conduct analytics to determine profitability and utilization of company resources. Based on the findings, be willing to act. Remember, understanding data is an art and a science. It is important to turn data into knowledge that supports actionable choices.

Meet with customers' leadership teams to re-evaluate those relationships that are a drag on the business and determine appropriate next steps for all parties. Work together to improve operational performance, enhance timelines, and reduce costs to improve margins while meeting customers' business needs. Develop plans with targeted milestones. Work together to deliver products that achieve their business objectives and support your business plan to improve the relationships for both organizations involved. If that is not possible, then be willing to act. Work together with your internal staff to sunset those customer relationships.

Can your leadership team articulate the performance of your key customer accounts? Do they and you genuinely understand the value of the books of business held by each account executive or customer engagement manager? When implementing and leading internal books of business review meetings, I witness many corporate leadership teams move away from pushing sales and organic growth targets on the account teams without a profound understanding of customers' business plans and strategies. After all, a client merging with another company may present growth opportunities or decide to cancel your contract and engage with another organization. A clear understanding of what is happening with your significant customers enables better financial forecasting and budgeting. It provides the opportunity to plan for expansion to support your customers' growing businesses.

Announcing sales and organic growth targets without these considerations is like driving a race car blindly to the finish line. There will probably be accidents along the way.

If not already established, consider implementing comprehensive book of business review meetings to create awareness among leadership teams and other staff, solidifying internal recognition of customers as corporate assets. The sessions establish a format for discussion and can identify internal political roadblocks that negatively impact organic growth and customer satisfaction. Executing appropriate action plans to improve performance and encouraging collaboration across business units is key to successful outcomes. Book of business review meetings can stimulate discussions regarding innovation and product development.

So, how do you make everything about them, so much so that in the end, it all circles back and becomes about the success of the company? **The answer is in your disciplined approach to leading the company by focusing on the business plan and customer lifecycles and fostering the company culture you desire to be successful.**

So, who owns customer relationships?

I often ask this question as I meet with business executives to assess the underlying causes of their business and customer retention challenges. This is a question that many of them struggle to answer completely. Frequently, I discover a need for more consensus among members of executive leadership teams as to who truly owns the management of their company's key account relationships. Do ownership and ultimate accountability reside with the chief executive officer, the chief revenue officer, the account executive, the consulting engagement leader, the customer success officer, the chief operations officer, or someone else? When executive leadership teams have difficulty answering this question, imagine how their staff answers the same question. Confusion, inefficiencies, and account retention challenges occur when business leaders need to invest in clearly defined business relationship management leadership and processes.

Retention and management of complex business relationships should be clearly defined with accountability for successes and loss of assets.

Key accounts are corporate assets. To enhance contract retention and organic growth, assign business relationship managers to each significant account. Successful business relationship managers assess their customers' business environments and invest in understanding their business strategies. They work with their customers to establish mutual goals and objectives. They are empowered, accountable, and appropriately compensated for the retention and growth of significant corporate assets. They are business-savvy individuals who are often responsible for books of business representing significant top-line revenue and margin. Essentially, they manage strategic business relationships that dramatically impact stakeholder value on both sides of the relationship equation. Successful business leaders recognize that these corporate assets should be protected and are willing to invest the necessary funds and resources to protect them.

Integrated teams with strategies and communication plans are critical to the success of longer-term relationships.

It is best to align team members with customer representatives based on mutual areas of responsibility. Successful business relationship managers orchestrate internal team meetings to communicate short-term and longer-term goals and objectives of the assets within their books of business. Team members monitor progress, identify current and potential issues, and develop appropriate action plans. Annual customer review meetings ensure that customers and business leaders acknowledge the value of their business relationships, identify challenges and solutions, and share accountability for progress. Stakeholder communications are necessary to avoid finger-pointing and establish accountability on both sides.

Implement a clearly defined and repeatable process to manage significant customer relationships and demonstrate value to achieve customers' business objectives. What do I mean by a repeatable process? It is important to establish a consistent approach to managing and monitoring books of business. Require quarterly book of business review meetings with the executive leadership team led by the assigned business relationship managers to review their significant customers' business goals and objectives and monitor progress. Establish business plans for each critical customer relationship, including organic growth and contract renewal metrics as needed to support annual books of business goals.

Suppose you tell me your company already creates account plans for each key customer. Can you confirm the account plans are created by collaborating with the customers to understand their business needs? Or are the account plans merely drafted based on desired organic growth goals without genuinely understanding customer needs and their unique business challenges? Companies that identify customer challenges and areas for performance improvement focus on customer longevity. They establish metrics to monitor problem resolutions. They listen to their customers to identify and discuss possible innovations and new product development initiatives to address changing customer needs and new competitive entrants in the market.

Understanding customers' business strategies provides valuable insight into their plans for growth, mergers, and acquisitions that can dramatically impact your revenue and staffing to support them. How would a key customer's pending merger impact your business if the merger doubled the customer's size or possibly resulted in contract termination? This information is essential when developing account plans to grow revenue and sustain customer loyalty. As earlier stated, establishing organic growth goals without knowing customers' business objectives is like blindly driving a race car to the finish line. There will probably be accidents.

Implementing internal executive business review meetings reveals progress and challenges in securing each corporate asset.

This approach enables business leaders to participate in developing and implementing appropriate action plans. This process can also enhance the accuracy of corporate revenue forecasting, strategic planning, and budgeting.

Front and center is the individual ultimately responsible for the success and loss of critical assets. Have you invested in people, processes, and technology to protect these corporate assets? Does your executive leadership team understand your customer's business environments and their business objectives? Truly?

Do you have a well-defined customer lifecycle model? Can you draw a diagram of the model and identify accountabilities between the company and your customers? Can your leadership team and managers draw the customer lifecycle model representing your business?

What is the customer experience? Is it easy or challenging to do business with your organization? Can you answer this question with confidence? Investigate processes. Identify processes to eliminate or improve to enhance customer satisfaction and ease of conducting business with your company.

Has your leadership team developed relationships with executive leaders within your key customer organizations? Do they add value to the relationships by consulting and collaborating with customers to collectively address changing market dynamics?

Have you established and confirmed how you and your customers want your business relationships to exist and evolve short term and longer term?

How do you work together today so that both sides of the table win in a challenging economy? The executive leadership team must demonstrate to your key customers that you understand their business needs and how your products and services meet their objectives. How do your customers measure success?

Within your organization, how do staff work together across functional teams to work together on behalf of the customer? Can customer engagement managers and account executives orchestrate internal resources to achieve expected deliverables on time and without error? Can they get things done, or do you have layers of bureaucracy they must navigate?

Have you fostered a culture that empowers everyone to deliver on customer expectations, or do you have turf wars and a highly political environment?

Answering these questions and implementing a comprehensive approach to managing complex customer relationships is the first step in protecting your company's most important assets.

TEAM COACHING YIELDS HIGH-PERFORMANCE RESULTS

Professional sports teams are big business. In the National Football League (NFL), the average salary for a head coach is about $7,000,000. A Major League Baseball (MLB) pitching coach makes between $200,000 and $400,000 annually. In both leagues, professional players bring significant experience and receive remarkably high salaries, yet they practice hard during training camps and the playing season. **They are**

successful because, as talented as they are, they all have incredible coaches and constantly work to improve their performance.

Coaches create their game day plan before game day. NFL coaches analyze opponents' game videos, and players study their opponents before game day. They all invest tremendous time preparing for the game. In addition to pre-planning for game day, coaches are on the football field sidelines and in the dugouts coaching their players before every gameplay. **Yet, those teams or players would only set foot on a football field or baseball diamond with their head coach, the coaching staff, and a game day plan.**

Millions of people—and the media—are watching on game day. Talk about pressure. Professional sports teams and their coaches receive immediate performance reviews from fans and the press, who scrutinize every play and every action on the field. Feedback is instantaneous. But that kind of feedback is not valuable coaching. Professional sports team owners depend on recruiting outstanding coaches who develop strong relationships between coaches and players to produce winning seasons and championships. They pay big bucks for the best coaches and coaching staff. What would the results be if coaches stayed in their offices and watched the games on TV? What would happen if the coaching staff reported the stats to the owner after every game? What would happen if NFL or MLB head coaches walked onto the team locker rooms and said, "You need to achieve this number of home runs this season, or you need to score this number of touchdowns and field goals this season," then walked out of the locker room and expected their teams to deliver the results. Imagine that!

Learning from the big business of professional sports, beyond the playing field and training camps, can be beneficial. I'm amazed at the number of companies that need to invest in leaders who are genuine revenue and business relationship management coaches.

Consider your business. Do your chief revenue officer and their sales management staff provide coaching in the field for individual sales and account executive team members? What coaching are they doing in the field to improve individual staff performance? Are they collaborating with staff to pre-plan each sales call? Does your company have a sustainable and consistent process for sales coaching led by sales and account management leadership to increase the performance of your sales and account executive professionals? Are you invested in account management leadership coaching to drive organic growth and retention of profitable business relationships?

Think about your chief revenue officer, account management, general manager, or chief customer experience officer. Are they sitting in senior leadership meetings reporting stats that include trends, sales updates, and customer contract renewal numbers? Are they conducting staff meetings where they deliver the message and mandate annual sales and organic growth quotas from their teams? Or are they truly engaged in weekly field coaching with their highly skilled staff to enable them to increase performance and develop their teams into actual revenue and business relationship management champions? Is your senior leadership providing weekly reporting on their coaching progress? Are your sales and account management leaders effective coaches?

Many companies invest in training salespeople and account executives, assuming the leaders know how to provide effective coaching. The reality is that leaders often need to learn how to coach effectively, and even worse, we find that leaders from the same company disagree on a standard definition of a quality sale call.

How can effective coaching occur without that agreement? Imagine if professional sports coaches could not agree on how to coach and develop their teams or game-day plan. Do you need to invest in coaching? Consider your business lifecycle. A disciplined approach to following the business plan is essential to achieving that handshake and developing a customer portfolio that supports the plan and achieves results. **To be effective, make it about them.**

Focus On a Well-Balanced Customer Portfolio

Maintaining a well-balanced customer portfolio that supports a recalibrated business plan can be challenging. When customer lifecycle management focuses on integrating the company's business plan with an ideal customer portfolio, the outcome is purposeful and dramatic. The business plan represents the current and future state of the business. Have you considered the impact on the customer portfolio and the customer lifecycle?

As market dynamics evolve, customer expectations and new product requirements emerge. The ability to generate profitable revenue and solidify the longevity of ideal customer relationships is vital for the success of a recalibrated business plan. As leadership updates the business plan, you may retire products or service offerings that are wasting resources and reducing profits that are no longer viable in supporting the new strategy. Achieving this goal may require short-term changes to products and services while the business simultaneously invests in innovation and new product development and implements new operational processes.

Managing the retirement of products that support current customers' business objectives can be challenging for business relationship management teams. Consider that your customers have specific goals and objectives supported by the company's existing product and service offerings. Not all current customers will be interested in the new developments in the company's innovation pipeline. With planning, collaboration, and effective management, existing customers who embrace the latest products and services can become future brand ambassadors.

Conduct analytics and develop champions to support the desired customer portfolio.

The team managing customer relationships must know about the business plan to manage their books of business against the plan's goals. It is essential to conduct periodic reviews of the customer portfolio to identify the business relationships that will prevail along with the company's short-term and long-term plans.

With assistance from the financial analytics staff, the business relationship management staff are the best qualified to provide the portfolio analysis. **The customer portfolio should evolve, reflecting the business's current and desired future state.**

Creating awareness with customer relationship management teams regarding required changes in the customer portfolio, including timelines to achieve business objectives short-term and long-term, is imperative for the success of the plan. Collaborating and communicating with the business relationship managers is essential to develop champions who believe and can drive performance with the new plan.

The customer portfolio analysis results may indicate the need to dissolve targeted customer relationships as your leadership team recalibrates the business to focus on more innovative products, leading to a new portfolio of more sophisticated customers. Requiring business relationship management teams to retire targeted customers within their books of business can take a lot of work to execute.

Business relationship management teams typically focus on customer retention and organic growth. The staff has specific revenue targets associated with their compensation. Asking them to dissolve segments of their existing pipeline and begin to focus on new products and service offerings while retiring current customers can impact their compensation. If so, work with staff to prepare account plans and timelines to sunset the accounts without disrupting the business and replace the lost revenue with customers more closely aligned with the ideal customer profiles. Collaboration with the account executives, customer engagement managers, and the sales organization is critical to sustain the top-line revenue and promote growth without eroding staff. Remember, when you sunset accounts, you reduce the value of books of business until new customers are onboarded. Account loss typically impacts staff compensation and causes them to explore new opportunities with your competition. The loss of intellectual capital that floats to the competition can damage your business.

Communication regarding new product launches and book of business management is essential for the timely execution of the plan. It is important to address new customer portfolio requirements with the sales organization and to address existing and future compensation based on portfolio metrics and timelines.

Communicating with the sales organization regarding the new business plan strategy and revised ideal customer profiles is crucial in redefining the future state of the overall customer portfolio.

Remember, customer lifecycle management begins with sales. It starts with the handshake. As new customers are onboarded, business relationship managers must appropriately manage their evolving books of business to drive profitable growth and retention of key accounts while keeping a well-balanced portfolio representing the company's future state.

Communication with key customers regarding the company's plan, including insight into innovation and product development initiatives, can prove beneficial. Does your company engage with your key customers' leadership teams? Meeting with customers' senior leaders can provide much-needed information regarding their roadmap for success and how your plan fits with their future business needs. Schedule annual customer executive staff meetings to demonstrate value and high-level interest in business relationships. Alignment between your organizations can create future disruptions in market dynamics by driving innovation forward and solidifying renewed customer contracts and growth.

It's about communication. It's about developing internal champions.

It's about you!

CHAPTER 6
HOUSEKEEPING THE PROCESSES

DO OPERATIONAL PROCESSES NEED POLISHING?

This chapter addresses the impact of implementing annual business process improvement (BPI) initiatives that provide a safe environment for collaboration across business unit verticals and ultimately improve customer satisfaction scores, retention, and organic growth.

DO OPERATIONAL PROCESSES NEED POLISHING?

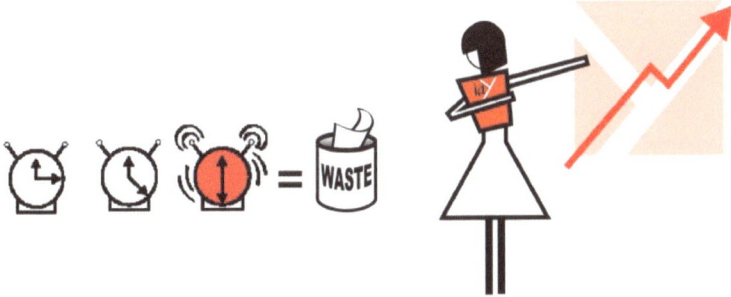

Business process improvement (BPI) can significantly enhance customer satisfaction, positively impact profits, upgrade communication across business unit verticals, and reduce rework by improving operational efficiencies. It may be time to investigate internal processes. Is your business experiencing a decline in contract renewals? Are you learning about delays and missed customer deadlines? Are your customer satisfaction scores indicating lower satisfaction rates? It may be time for your leadership team to investigate the processes within their vertical organizations.

Chapter 3 was about culture and its impact on the success of the business plan. Does your corporate culture foster teamwork and collaboration across business units, or is it highly political and resistant to collaboration and change? Because business units rely on each other to achieve deadlines on time and within budget, project plans and cross-functional processes can provide insight into areas needing revisions.

Learn from the frontline.

Business process improvement (BPI) can provide a safe environment for staff to engage in candid conversations regarding operational processes that need improvements within their business units. Frontline staff typically have the most helpful insight into where to find inefficiencies. The outcome can be fantastic when individuals are encouraged and empowered to describe and implement their recommendations. After all, the people who do the work know what needs to be changed to make things more efficient.

Listen to your staff and act.

- Communicate the approved changes with each business unit.

- Retrain staff to ensure successful implementation within and across business unit verticals.

- Engage the internal audit organization to confirm new processes are implemented and followed.

- Identify and communicate key performance indicators (KPIs) and metrics to monitor the impact of new processes. Regularly review KPIs and metrics. Check with staff periodically to see if re-calibration is needed to achieve results.

- Provide staff with positive feedback regarding milestones achieved.

- Communicate improvements to customers and listen to their feedback.

It's about listening and acting.
It's about you!

CHAPTER 7
THE SIGNIFICANCE OF TYING IT ALL TOGETHER

IT BEGINS WITH THE BUSINESS PLAN

IT'S ALL IMPACTED BY YOUR WILLINGNESS TO ACT

This chapter reviews the value of focusing on the basics, improving market position, and sustaining growth. Regardless of the size of the company, the challenges are all the same.

It Begins with the Business Plan

By now, you should agree that business success begins with a well-defined and current business plan appropriately communicated to employees. Company culture directly impacts the efficient execution of the plan and achieving the desired results. Keeping a pulse on changing market dynamics and evolving regulatory requirements can affect new product development and innovation timeliness. Understanding and defining the business and customer lifecycle models unique to your organization provides the foundation for plan discipline, solidifies awareness of processes within each stage of the lifecycles, and provides the format for effective knowledge transfer regarding accountability for customers' business objectives, strategies, expected timelines, and deliverables.

Although you may have seasoned sales and account management teams, Sales leaders must provide in-field coaching to improve performance, something many sales leaders overlook. It is important to keep staff focused on delivering within the guidelines of the plan to sustain the desired customer portfolio.

Customer relationships are corporate assets to be nurtured and protected. Providing clarity and purpose regarding ownership of customer relationships is critical for retention and organic growth. Maintaining a customer portfolio that supports the business plan and strategy short term and long term is a critical success factor and not easy to do. It requires periodic analytics and a deep understanding of existing customer relationships and how your products and services support their business objectives. Retiring products or divesting business units can impact customer relationships. Be aware of the potential financial impact.

Assessing relationships that drag on the business is essential to orchestrate either account plans to improve financial and operational performance or develop plans to exit the relationships without negatively impacting your position within the industry.

Declining contract renewals and missed project deadlines indicate operational processes need reviewing. Investigate by implementing companywide systematic business process improvement (BPI) initiatives that can highlight operational successes, provide insight into opportunities for improved efficiencies, and provide a safe format to enhance collaboration across business unit verticals. Follow up on implemented changes. Retrain staff and sustain the new processes. Engage the internal audit team to confirm the implementation of the new processes within the desired timelines. Communicate the improvements to customers and listen to feedback. Monitor the segments of the customer lifecycle model and track future contract renewals. Of course, many things impact customer longevity; BPI is only one of those factors.

It's All Impacted by Your Willingness to Act

Focusing on the basics requires a willingness for leadership to act. It is just that simple. The basics never change, but leadership teams do. So, if you have a change in executive leadership positions, keep an eye on the leadership verticals and changes within the company culture. Review the business and customer lifecycle models for necessary periodic updates. Require in-field sales and account management team coaching to enhance performance and maintain plan discipline. Conduct internal book of business review meetings quarterly to keep a pulse on key customer relationships and identify innovation opportunities to support customers' evolving business needs and strategies. Meet with customers' executive teams annually to demonstrate value, collaborate regarding mutual business objectives, and protect key corporate assets.

CHAPTER 8
WHY IT WORKS

WHEN YOU MAKE IT ABOUT THEM, IT'S ALL ABOUT YOU!

This is not rocket science. It is simple and basic.
But often, the basics are overlooked because leaders
are too busy, the business is performing well, or leaders are
uncertain of the real issues. So, they fail to appropriately
pause, investigate, and make necessary changes.

Success is truly about your leadership and style!
Changing things you can, does require effort.
Doing nothing is a choice.
People and relationships are complex.
Make it about Them,
Then it's all about You!

ACKNOWLEDGMENTS

Cover and graphics

Dianne Stucky, Founder, Graphic Designer, Illustrator

Off the Wall Pen & Ink Creations
Penninkcreations.com

Website design - It's About You Business Consulting SM, LLC

IAYConsulting.com

Sharon Sweeney

Illume Marketing
Illumemarketing.com

Editing, print interior design, and ebook design

JETLAUNCH.net

ABOUT THE AUTHOR

As founder of It's About You Business Consulting℠, LLC...

Michelle Jahn is a seasoned sales and marketing executive with over twenty-five years of experience successfully developing innovative business models and achieving exceptional results. As founder of It's About You Business Consulting ℠, LLC, she has worked with Fortune 100 companies and companies in the US, Europe, and Canada implementing models for customer lifecycle management, leading and coaching sales organizations, and new product launches.

Michelle has held key senior leadership positions at numerous companies, including MedImpact Healthcare Systems, Inc., where she was SVP responsible for client retention and 20% (YOY) growth of the nationwide client portfolio. She also led annual company-wide business process improvement (BPI) initiatives that improved operational efficiencies and client implementation processes. As the Sr. Advisor and international business development executive, she provided sales coaching for global regions and senior leadership oversight for new products for Canada.

Other career highlights include her work at Chronimed, Inc. (BioScrip/Option Care), where she provided executive leadership for the successful integration and reorganization of the company's nationwide specialty retail pharmacy and mail order sales, increasing sales by 33% in the first year. At Caremark, Inc (CVS Caremark), Michelle received the President's Club Award for national account management. Promoted to Caremark corporate sales, she developed sales strategies to increase product penetration in the Midwest region.

At Vivius, Inc., an early-stage consumer-directed healthcare company, she served as executive vice president and chief marketing officer, where she led sales, marketing, advertising, and media relations. She became the interim vice president of commercial sales for Health Spring, a Vivius client in Nashville, TN, where she delivered a comprehensive assessment of the sales strategy and improved sales performance for the health plan.

Michelle worked at Baxter International, Management Services Division, generating the top sales of modeling and forecasting software products for strategic planning and marketing to hospital executives in the Midwest and Mid-Atlantic regions. She developed a successful physician practice marketing program for a 450-bed teaching hospital in a highly competitive market in Ohio and was a pioneer in the early development of the viatical settlement industry in the US.

Her clinical experience as a respiratory therapist included developing a comprehensive education and rehabilitation program for pulmonary disease. She provided hospital-based clinical instruction at Mercy Medical Center (Cleveland Clinic Mercy Hospital) for the University of Akron's pulmonary rehab program. She was also responsible for the hospital-owned cardiopulmonary service in a rural community providing services that enhanced access to outpatient care.

Throughout her career, Michelle has shown a strong commitment to the community. Several Board of Director positions included Chair and President of Mama's Kitchen in San Diego (CA), where she provided key leadership during the coronavirus pandemic. Under her leadership, the organization continued to support vulnerable individuals and families by serving over 10 million medically tailored meals to seriously ill San Diegans.

You are invited to visit the website **IAYconsulting.com**.

You may contact Michelle Jahn via email or on the website.

Her email is **Michelle.Jahn@IAYconsulting.com**.